This book is protected by the great goddess Kali and belongs to:

Don't mess with her—take my word for it.

Namaste

The Little Book of

Hindu

deities

From the Goddess of Wealth
to the Sacred Cow

**Written & Illustrated
by Sanjay Patel**

A PLUME BOOK

Dedicated to
One Orange **Giraffe**

PLUME
Published by Penguin Group

Penguin Group (USA) Inc., 375 Hudson Street, New York, New York
10014, U.S.A. • Penguin Group (Canada), 90 Eglinton Avenue East, Suite
700, Toronto, Ontario, Canada M4P 2Y3 (a division of Pearson Penguin
Canada Inc.) • Penguin Books Ltd., 80 Strand, London WC2R 0RL, England
• Penguin Ireland, 25 St. Stephen's Green, Dublin 2, Ireland (a division of
Penguin Books Ltd.) • Penguin Group (Australia), 250 Camberwell Road,
Camberwell, Victoria 3124, Australia (a division of Pearson Australia
Group Pty. Ltd.) • Penguin Books India Pvt. Ltd., 11 Community Centre,
Panchsheel Park, New Delhi – 110 017, India • Penguin Books (NZ), cnr
Airborne and Rosedale Roads, Albany, Auckland 1310, New Zealand (a
division of Pearson New Zealand Ltd.) • Penguin Books (South Africa) (Pty.)
Ltd., 24 Sturdee Avenue, Rosebank, Johannesburg 2196, South Africa

Penguin Books Ltd., Registered Offices:
80 Strand, London WC2R 0RL, England

First published by Plume, a member of Penguin Group (USA) Inc.
First Printing, November 2006
21
Copyright © Sanjay Patel, 2006
All rights reserved

℗ REGISTERED TRADEMARK—MARCA REGISTRADA
CIP data is available.
ISBN 0-452-28775-8
Printed in the United States of America
Set in Myriad Pro
Book design by Sanjay Patel

Ladoos (Sweets)

Gods of India

Who knew there were so many gods?

INTRODUCTION

When I was a kid growing up in L.A., it was my job every morning to go outside and pick fresh marigolds with bright orange petals for my father. I would collect enough to fill the large round steel thali (dinner plate). After washing them, I would add a little bit of water to the thali to keep the flowers fresh and carefully carry them inside to my father. His bedroom was filled with the smell of incense and the low sound of an old devotional song coming from a small tape player. My father would already be showered and looking fresh, sitting on the ground on a small mat in front of his mandir (temple). Before I approached the mandir, I was always mindful to take off my shoes so as not to offend my dad—or the gods. This temple was comprised of a large open bookshelf filled with small murtis (idols of the gods) and framed prints of **Shiva**, **Vishnu**, and **Durga**, all lined by small diyas (candles). As I handed the plate of flowers to my dad, I knew my job was done and his would just be beginning. He had a row of fresh rolled wicks made of cotton and dunked in oil that he would place in the small round cup waiting to be lit in devotion to the gods. He would then meticulously wash each murti and mix red powder and water to apply a small dab of red paste to each god's forehead. He finished by picking off a single flower petal and sticking it to the wet paste. The result was an array of gods and goddesses all glimmering by the light of the diyas with an array of bright orange flower petals pasted to their foreheads. My dad would then commence a puja (religious ritual) by ringing a brass bell and singing devotional songs to summon the gods to the offering he had made. Only after the gods had been properly fed and bathed did my dad start to make a pot of chai tea for my mother and himself.

There was one big bonus to waking up early to help my dad: cartoons. Specifically, I liked Japanese cartoons like *Voltron* and *Robotech*. I would sit glued to the TV as long as possible until it was time to go off to school. By the time I got back home in the afternoon, it was American cartoons like *Looney Tunes*, *GI Joe*, and *Transformers* that held my imagination, and when the cartoons were over, I would pore over comics and draw from them—this was my nirvana. As I got older I never lost the passion for drawing or animation, so I enrolled at CalArts in the character animation department. In two short years, I was recruited by Pixar. The art of animation merges many powerful disciplines, but I always gravitated toward storytelling and design—which are the perfect tools to retell the Hindu mythology.

Hindu imagery is a feast of storytelling, design, and philosophy. But as I was growing up, I saw it as a mystery of people and animals that made no sense. Being raised in the East-West culture clash, I was exposed to Hinduism through my parents' best efforts, but they were met by my lack of interest due to my frustration with trying to fit in. I'm what some might call ABCD, American-born confused Desi (Indian), though I was actually born in the United Kingdom. I have no formal education in Hindu mythology beyond what my family exposed me to. It was only after I started drawing Hindu gods that I started to ask serious questions. This is where my informal education of Hinduism began and the confusion started to clear. I examined books full of vivid miniature paintings of Hindu mythology and would draw my own versions of them. Gradually I started to read about my favorite gods and goddesses, was entertained by their exploits, and began to understand what they have come to symbolize. The more I read and researched, the more inspired I was to draw, and before I knew it, I was well on my way to creating this book.

I've tried to take a fun and lighthearted approach to designing these gods. This mythology is the source of deep religious belief for millions of people and, with this in mind, I've treaded very carefully and looked to create the most harmless and joyful designs possible. I quickly made a connection with Sanrio's ultracute Hello Kitty designs and thought, "Well, there's a style that no one could get offended by." My first experiment was "chunky monkey," a drawing I did of a plump Hanuman flying in the air. I showed it to my wife, and she shook her head with a big smile on her face. From there I drew Shiva surrounded by cute cobras that looked more like worms and Krishna playing his flute. But it was designing the more frightening aspects of Hinduism that I had the most fun with, such as the goddess Kali and her dual aspects of fear and comfort. She may be carrying the head of her victim, but she has an innocent smile that's also sort of disarming and comforting. It's my sincere hope that these designs and explanations pique people's curiosity and help them make a fun connection to the ancient mythologies of Hinduism.

Sanjay Patel
3-26-06

11

GANESHA BLESSING

Ganesha was granted a very special gift to make up for the fact that he had an elephant's head. His gift was that no one would begin important endeavors or pujas (religious rituals) without seeking Ganesha's blessing first. Carrying on in the Hindu tradition, *The Little Book of Hindu Deities* starts by honoring and introducing Ganesha.

GANESHA

(guh-NAY-shuh)

Ganesha is the eldest son of Shiva and his wife, Parvati, and he is the lord of all living things. He became lord when he beat his brother, Karttikeya, in a race around the universe. Instead of bolting across the earth like his brother did, Ganesha simply circled his parents—the sources of life—to win the race. There are many stories that explain how Ganesha came to have the head of an elephant. One says that his mother created Ganesha out of dirt to protect her while Shiva was away. When Shiva came home to see his wife, Ganesha refused him entry, not realizing who Shiva was, and in anger Shiva cut off his son's head. In a panic to appease his distraught wife, Shiva brought Ganesha back to life and gave him the head of an elephant. It wasn't a perfect match, but Ganesha's elephant ears have served him well, the better to hear the needs of his people. Ganesha brings good luck and also clears obstacles, as symbolized by the ax he carries. For these reasons he is worshipped before important events and rituals. Ganesha also has a sweet tooth, so be sure to share your ladoos (sweets) with him.

TRIMURTI (try-MOOR-tee)

In Hinduism, God is thought to be made up of three gods. This holy trinity is known as the Trimurti. The three forms of this trinity are the gods Brahma, Vishnu, and Shiva. Hindus believe that the gods within the trinity represent the following three aspects: creation (Brahma); preservation (Vishnu); and destruction (Shiva). But we should not forget that behind all great gods there are great goddesses that assist them in their duties. These goddesses are the consorts of the Trimurti; they are Sarasvati, Lakshmi, and Parvati.

BRAHMA

(BRUH-ma)

A single day in Brahma's life lasts more than four million years. He is the creator of the world and all the living things upon it. It is said that when Brahma wanted to create the universe, he designed a goddess out of his own flesh and blood. She came to be known as Sarasvati. Being a shy goddess, Sarasvati was uncomfortable with Brahma's adoring eyes and tried to hide from his gaze. But each way she turned, Brahma sprouted a head so he could always watch her. In addition to having four heads, Brahma keeps his four hands busy grooming his long beards. Sometimes he rides a magical goose or white swan endowed with the ability to tell good from evil. Unlike other gods, Brahma carries no weapon, though he does keep a carafe of water with him at all times, and not just to quench his thirst—it contains the source of life. Brahma is also the keeper of the Holy Vedas, the books containing the story of how the world was created. Brahma's four faces are thought to represent the four Vedas, though you can only ever see three of his faces, since his fourth face is always behind him.

VISHNU

(VISH-noo)

It is said that good and evil forces are always battling for control of the world—the gods work to preserve the good, and the demons work to spread evil. Vishnu's role in the great trinity is that of the invincible protector. Generally, when all is going well, good and evil are in balance. When things fall into chaos, however, Vishnu takes a trip down to earth to preserve justice. Sometimes he comes as himself, a blue four-armed god, but he can also appear in the form of Matsya, Kurma, Varaha, Narasimha, Vamana, Parashurama, Rama, Krishna, Buddha, or Kalki. These are the ten incarnations, or avatars, of Vishnu. The most famous incarnations are his seventh, eighth, and ninth forms, Rama, Krishna, and Buddha. Vishnu is often depicted sleeping in the coils of a giant snake floating on a cosmic ocean, though he recommends that unless you're invincible, it's better to sleep in your own bed than on snakes.

SHIVA

(SHIV-ah)

Shiva is one of the oldest gods of India and plays many important roles. He is a devout meditator and yogi, a cosmic dancer setting the rhythms of the universe, a benevolent protector and husband, and part of the great Hindu trinity. Shiva is the god of destruction, transformation, and regeneration. As such, snakes and deer are often associated with Shiva, as they are able to shed their skin or grow new antlers. Shiva is often found meditating on top of the Himalayas, a place of pilgrimage for thousands of Hindus. Although Shiva likes to get away from it all, he is also husband to Parvati and father to Ganesha and Karttikeya, so he's got a pretty busy life. He might sport a loincloth and have long hippie hair, but he's still a responsible father— aside from that time he cut off Ganesha's head. Shiva usually has a trident stuck into the ground next to where he's sitting. The three tines of this pitchfork-type weapon correspond to the creation, protection, and destruction of the universe. At his other side, he has a drum so he can kick up his heels when he's done meditating. Some think that when Shiva finishes dancing, the world will come to an end—so keep the music coming! Shiva has long hair, but he is not a girl. He just doesn't like haircuts.

MANIFESTATIONS of SHIVA

Hindu gods are not strictly defined; they evolve organically to merge many ideologies as one. Shiva is narrowly defined within the Hindu trinity as a destructive force, but taken in isolation we see he is, in fact, a god with many faces and attributes. These aspects take shape as Shiva's manifestations from loving husband, nurturing father, and meditative yogi to terrifying protector. Depending on the circumstance, Shiva takes on a different form to protect his devotees.

UMA MAHESHVARA

(OO-ma muh-hesh-VAR-ah)

Shiva and his consort, Parvati, symbolize the yin and yang of nature. Parvati is also known as Uma, and Shiva is also known as Maheshvara. Together they are the inseparable one, known as Uma Maheshvara. Through Parvati, Shiva is able to manifest his full potential and express himself as a loving husband and caring father. Without her he would remain an isolated monk immersed in yoga meditation. Parvati not only complements Shiva, she completes him. According to myth, after their marriage, Shiva and Parvati went on a honeymoon that lasted many years, which irritated the gods to no end. The gods took it upon themselves to try and break up the two lovebirds, but whenever they tried to interrupt, Shiva would quickly expose the gods to the melting heat of his third eye. Eventually Shiva and Parvati emerged as a married couple with their children, Karttikeya (also known as Skanda) and Ganesha, making a home on Mount Kailash, in the Himalayas. The constant companion and vehicle of Lord Shiva and his family is the snow-white bull known as Nandi, on whom, it is thought, only those who have conquered their desires through yoga are fit to ride. Who needs a dog as a companion when you can ride a bull? That is, if you've done your yoga.

RUDRA

(ROO-drah)

Perhaps the first and oldest manifestation of Shiva is the god Rudra ("howler"). According to legend, Brahma, the god of creation, was once so angry that from his forehead sprang Rudra, who split into male and female forms, representing the perfect balance of the male and female energies. To the early Hindu practitioners, Rudra was a nature god who took out his vengeance through natural disasters. The Vedas have many references to Rudra's wrath and came to call him by many names: the roaring god, the terrible god, the god of storms, and the god of the tempest. No one was safe from Rudra; he brought sickness to gods, men, and animals. But to be fair, Rudra wasn't all bad. The Vedas also mention that if you were lucky enough to be on his good side, Rudra could be kind and generous. As Hinduism progressed over time, Rudra's destructive qualities merged with the traits of other beneficial gods of nature. Eventually, he came to be known as a caring god and as the lord of the animals and the patron of hunters. You can recognize Rudra by the antelope emerging from his hand and the ax carried by hunters in his other hand. This complex evolution—from wrathful primitive god to sympathetic icon of meditation—explains many of Shiva's contradictions.

BHAIRAVA

(bai-RUH-vuh)

Shiva has dozens of manifestations in his enraged aspect, but Bhairava is Shiva at his most terrifying. Bhairava is especially scary since he has the power to conjure up our own worst fears and force us to confront them. Bhairava appears before us naked and horrible, displaying his sharp fangs. It's no surprise that his name has become synonymous with fear—he is thought to be a manifestation of Shiva's anger and his vengeance toward Lord Brahma. According to legend, Brahma created a beautiful daughter and grew to have unnatural desires for her. Because he was so enamored with his own daughter, Brahma actually grew a fifth head so he could pay constant attention to her. But his daughter was suffocated by all of her father's attention and decided it would be better to die and move on to heaven than be shamed by her own father. Shiva was so offended by the creator's actions that his anger took on the terrifying shape of Bhairava and exacted vengeance on Brahma by cutting off one of his five heads. Brahma learned a painful lesson and ended his lust for his own creations. But since Brahma was actually Shiva's father, the beheading caused Bhairava great grief. Bhairava atoned for his sins by doing penance. He became a beggar and was cursed to use his father's decapitated skull as a begging bowl. For years Bhairava wandered in near blindness with Brahma's skull stuck to his hand. Only upon reaching the holy city of Benares did he receive forgiveness, and the begging bowl dropped from his hand. Bhairava does have some redeeming qualities. He is useful as a protector against harm and is still painted in villages to ward off evil spirits. But two wrongs don't make a right—so next time you're angry with your parents, don't turn into a monster.

NATARAJA

(NUH-tuh-rahj-uh)

One of the great symbols of Hinduism is Shiva's manifestation as Nataraja, the king of dancers. Nataraja's cosmic dance symbolizes the balance of the three aspects of the Hindu trinity—creation, preservation, and destruction—where opposites are intrinsically connected. To begin, Nataraja holds a small drum in his upper right hand from which creation is said to spring forth in the form of musical rhythm. His lower right hand forms a gesture of blessing, symbolizing preservation. The upper left hand holds a flame, which is thought to symbolize the destruction of life. Thus, the hand holding the drum and the one holding fire balance the forces of creation and destruction. The arm held across the chest gestures toward his raised foot as a promise of Nataraja's mercy and kindness to all his devotees. His other foot rests on a dwarf demon, which is thought to symbolize human cruelty and people's lack of respect for one another. Through his dance, Nataraja shows us how to achieve enlightenment; by forgetting yourself and losing hold of maya (illusion), you can finally be liberated from the cycle of death and rebirth. Who else but a god can manage to do so much while standing on only one foot?

LİNGAM

(LIN-gum)

It is important to note that the lingam is not a manifestation but an age-old symbol of Shiva. Due to Shiva's complex forms and aspects, a simple stone became the easiest way to worship him. The lingam can be found in almost all of Shiva's temples as the focal point of worship. Lingams are usually composed of stone, either carved or found already formed. Generally a smooth rounded stone is placed upright into a circular base known as a yoni. Together the stone and the base symbolize the union of man and woman, also known as Shiva and Shakti. The yoni typically has an inner ring that acts as a drain for water that is offered upon the lingam during ceremonies. Sometimes there is a hanging pot of water above it with a tiny hole in the bottom to allow a constant drip of water to fall upon the holy stone. The lingam is seen by many as a phallic symbol or as a sign of Shiva's fertile energy. This energy is thought to radiate heat, which is why water is offered upon it, to cool or calm the god's energy. Often the lingam is marked with three horizontal lines that represent the three aspects of the divine. During puja, Shiva devotees mark their own foreheads with three lines in sacred ash or sandalwood paste. Perhaps the next time you are skipping stones near a river, you might find a sign of Lord Shiva.

MOTHER GODDESS (Mahadevi)

Mahadevi is a complex figure and takes on many forms. Her early incarnations were associated with fertility and nature, such as the goddess Ganga, who later manifested herself as the life-sustaining river Ganges. Later Mahadevi became Shiva's benevolent and loving wife, Parvati, who matches her husband in her mastery of yoga. Finally, she became the ultimate goddess, appearing as a bloodthirsty warrior known as Durga and Kali.

SARASVATI

(suh-ruhs-VAH-tee)

Sarasvati is the goddess of knowledge and the arts. She has the proud status of being the first goddess to be worshipped in Hinduism and is a shining example for her younger siblings, Lakshmi and Parvati. Goddess Sarasvati, being wise and creative, was thought to be the perfect match for Brahma, the lord of creation. But according to some legends, Sarasvati and Brahma had a disastrous marriage. Put off by Sarasvati's lack of affection due to her being both his daughter and wife, Brahma chose to disinherit her and kick her out of his house. So much for divorce court. But this great insult didn't go unpunished. Brahma was subsequently cursed to lose his devotees and their worship in the temples. Thankfully, Sarasvati bounced back with a fabulous set of pearl mala (rosaries) to channel her anger through meditation, and went on to establish a unique identity. She developed a creative community of her own and has come to symbolize the independent woman as a thinker and a gifted creator. Though this goddess has no children, it is widely believed that musicians, artists, writers, and students are all part of her family and under her care. Free from a husband's nagging, Sarasvati enjoys playing her instrument, the veena, as loud as she wants and can sit glued to her favorite books, the Vedas, guilt-free for hours. She is a picture of grace and elegance, so it's little wonder that she chooses the beautiful white swan as her constant companion. Gods, eat your heart out, because this goddess is not available or interested—that is, unless you have a library card or can play back-up sitar.

DURGA

(DOOR-gah)

When the buffalo demon Mahish—rumored to be an invincible giant—and his army of demons threatened to push the gods out of heaven, the gods called a meeting to discuss how to get rid of him. Shiva suggested each god contribute a portion of his or her power to create a whole new being, the result of which was a new goddess whose face reflected the light of Shiva and who had six arms from Lord Vishnu and two feet from Lord Brahma. And so Durga was born, a powerful and pretty goddess. She is good-looking and fierce—a lethal combination! Before facing Mahish, Durga equipped herself with a sword, a club, and a chakra (discus). A fearless warrior, she easily defeated Mahish and restored balance to the world of the gods. With the name Durga, which means "invincible" in Sanskrit, she was kind of a shoe-in. In India, people celebrate Durga's victory over Mahish in one of their most important festivals, Durga Puja, which lasts ten days. But Durga isn't all fighting and no fun. Through her battles against suffering and injustice, she brings kindness and harmony. She is known to feed both people and animals, and is partial to riding around on big tigers or lions. And Durga is never afraid, not even in the dark.

LAKSHMI

(LAHK-shmee)

Beautiful Lakshmi is the goddess of wealth and happiness. When the gods were sent into exile, Lakshmi hid in the ocean of milk. It did wonders for her skin, but it wasn't as fun as being with the gods. Then, a great flood occurred, covering all of the earth. The gods came out of hiding and set up a huge game of tug-of-war with the demons below, each pulling their side to stir up some waves and hopefully reveal some of the precious things that were lost under the milk. One of those precious things was Lakshmi, who was reborn with a clear complexion during what became known as the churning of the ocean. When the gods saw Lakshmi emerge from the milk, they all fell in love with her. Shiva was the boldest and claimed her as his wife, but Lakshmi didn't want him. She wanted to be with Vishnu. How do you turn down one of the oldest gods of India? Luckily, Lakshmi didn't have to. Shiva had already taken Parvati as his wife, so Lakshmi became Vishnu's consort. She's never too far from his side and can often be found massaging his feet. Now that's love. When her hands aren't occupied rubbing her husband's tired toes, one of her four arms bestows gifts of prosperity; the others hold lotus flowers and the holy Aum symbol for well-being. Lakshmi is best known for good luck, but don't expect her to visit you at the slot machines. She has a really low tolerance for people who only desire her for money.

PARVATI

(par-VUH-tee)

Parvati is known by many names: Uma, Guari, and Shakti. She was born into royalty high in the Himalayas. According to legend, a priest came to her village when Parvati was a child and studied the marks on her body in order to predict her future. The priest concluded that Parvati would marry a great yogi. Parvati's royal parents were not happy at the prospect of their daughter marrying a poor yogi. But despite their efforts, they could not dissuade Parvati from falling in love with Shiva. Parvati resolved to win over the reclusive god. She visited Shiva's cave every day, filling it with flowers and fruits, hoping to win his love. But Shiva was steadfast in his meditation, never once casting his gaze upon her lovely face. Exasperated, the goddess decided to fight fire with fire and took retreat in the forest. She went into an extended meditative state to create so much concentrated energy that Shiva would find it impossible to ignore her. Eventually, Parvati's plan worked, as her energy became so great that Shiva's meditation was interrupted and he stepped out of his cave to accept her as his wife. Parvati's commitment to Lord Shiva is seen as the ideal of the unflappable Hindu wife and devotee. She is also the nurturing mother of two children, Ganesha and Karttikeya, who became great gods in their own right.

SITA

(SEE-tah)

From the very beginning Sita was quite special, as she was literally made from the earth. She was discovered as a baby, divinely born in a furrow of a plowed field, which is why she is thought of as the daughter of the earth goddess. But this farm girl is no country bumpkin. Her saga of abduction and devotion, in the epic story the Ramayana, has inspired India throughout the ages. Sita, an avatar of goddess Lakshmi, was the central love interest of Prince Rama (the seventh incarnation of Vishnu). According to legend, Sita was abducted and imprisoned by the demon king Ravana. After being imprisoned for months in Ravana's palace, Sita was finally rescued by Rama and his army. Returning to their rightful kingdom, Rama and Sita ushered in an era of peace and prosperity. However, within Rama's court a rumor emerged questioning Sita's chastity during her capture. For the sake of peace in his kingdom, Rama gave in to the rumors and, as pressure mounted, rejected Sita. Finding no other way to prove herself, Sita walked into a blazing fire to prove her purity. Astonishingly, the god of fire, Agni, did not harm her. Sita returned to Rama intact, but he again put his kingdom's wishes ahead of his own and rejected her loyalty. Tired of Rama's priorities and the injustice of the world, she asked for sanctuary with the earth goddess. All the gods watched as the earth split open, allowing Sita to descend deep within, never to return. Sita's martyrdom to her duty as a steadfast and faithful wife has left a profound legacy.

KALI

(KAH-lee)

Kali, the "Black One," is said to have shot from Durga's forehead when the protecting goddess was in a rage, and so she takes the form of the great goddess at her most terrifying. Just looking at her is enough to give you nightmares. She has four arms, a third red eye, and a belt made of human hands. In one hand, she carries the head of a demon, in two others, her weapons of destruction—a sickle and a sword. To complete her skimpy ensemble, she wears a necklace made of skulls, which is one of the few things covering her naked body. Though the fiercest of the gods, Kali is quite often mistaken as the goddess of death (this is actually the Hindu god Yama's responsibility). She is, in fact, the goddess of kala (time) and is thought to end our illusions and free us from the cycle of karma by bringing us liberation from our bodies. Her role is profound, as she is responsible for making sure that all things die in order to continue the cycle of life. Kali's blood-dripping tongue symbolizes her great victory over the demon Raktabija, who was extra hard to kill because the blood from each wound Kali inflicted spawned a new demon. But quick-witted Kali solved the dilemma by drinking the demon's blood so that not a drop could spill. She then swallowed his whole body in one quick bite. What can you say? Some girls have big appetites. It is important to note that Kali vanquished this demon in order to protect her devotees, who regard her as a loving mother goddess, not a killer. Kali also works part-time making sure everyone gets the measles and the mumps so their bodies can be stronger when they need to fight other germs.

TEN AVATARS of VISHNU (Dashavatar)

The great god Vishnu is seen as the protector of the universe. Vishnu descended to earth ten times as various avatars whenever the earth was threatened by evil. His avatars followed an evolutionary pattern, from fish and reptile through mammals and men and finally to the future creator. It is through his avatars that Vishnu maintains his role as the great preserver of creation.

MATSYA

(mut-SYE-yah)

Vishnu's first incarnation is in the form of an enormous fish known as Matsya. In this form Vishnu saved the four Vedas from being lost forever in the great flood. It all started when the lord of creation, Brahma, started to fall asleep. That would have been really bad, since if Brahma ever falls asleep, it would bring forth the Pralaya (Brahma's night), and the universe as we know it would come to an end. As Brahma drifted off, an asura (demon) named Hayagriva decided to take advantage of the sleepy god and steal the Vedas from him. But Vishnu saw Hayagriva take the holy books and descend into the ocean. Vishnu quickly took the form of Matsya and dove deep into the blue water. He swam until he came upon Hayagriva and vanquished the demon easily with his enormous bulk and a crushing blow from his mighty tail fin. Vishnu then grabbed the sacred Vedas and raced to the surface to deliver them to Brahma. As the Pralaya was fast approaching, signaling an end to all life on earth, Vishnu had just enough time to save one special person from the ocean waters. Luckily he picked Manu, the forefather of mankind, whom he dragged across the sea in a conch shell and kept safe until the ocean finally calmed down and creation could begin again. Matsya is something of a lifeguard for humans and books, but he doesn't recommend reading underwater.

KURMA

(KOOR-muh)

The second avatar of Vishnu is Kurma, the strong turtle. In the ongoing battles between the devatas (gods) and asuras (demons), there was once an occasion when the gods suddenly lost all their strength due to a curse. The devatas approached Vishnu for help. He advised them to retrieve the amrita (the nectar of immortality) from the flooded earth by churning the primitive ocean of milk using a mountain as a churning stick. Vishnu knew that the devatas alone couldn't move a mountain and advised them to seek help from their enemy, the asuras, in exchange for a share of the precious nectar. Working together, they used the giant serpent Vasuki as a rope to tie around the great mountain to help turn it and whip up the ocean. But as the churning proceeded, the mountain began sinking into the ocean. Noticing the sinking mountain, Lord Vishnu quickly took the form of the turtle Kurma. Crawling underneath the mountain, Kurma was able to keep the mountain afloat by supporting it upon his strong shell. But as soon as the amrita surfaced, the asuras grabbed it and wouldn't share it with the devatas. Vishnu quickly used his great power and seduced the asuras into serving the nectar to the devatas first, leaving not one drop for the greedy demons. Fueled by the nectar, the devatas regained their powers and were once again able to hold their own against the demons.

VARAHA

(vuh-RAH-huh)

The rugged boar is the third incarnation of Vishnu. According to Indian legend, after the great flood of Pralaya, as Brahma was busy creating a new universe, the earth goddess Bhoomdevi was stolen by the horrible demon Hiranyaksha, who not only stole the earth but hid Bhoomdevi deep within the cosmic ocean of creation. All the gods were outraged by this atrocity and commenced a holy fire ritual to summon Lord Vishnu. Quickly realizing the gravity of the situation, Vishnu transformed himself into a giant boar and dove deep into the cosmic ocean. The boar's giant nostrils and powerful sense of smell helped him search every corner of the ocean until he found the earth, hooked it on his tusks, and carried it back to the surface. On the way, he ran into Hiranyaksha, who was looking for a fight and thought the boar would be no match for him. But the poor demon didn't stand a chance against the divine boar, as Varaha rammed Hiranyaksha in one powerful thrust and brought an end to his stealing of planets. The earth goddess Bhoomdevi was saved and sanctified by the great preserver's touch. The trip through the soup of creation also left the planet washed and fertile, and helped create a suitable home for mankind.

NARASIMHA

(nuh-ruh-SIM-huh)

After the great boar Varaha destroyed Hiranyaksha, his brother, King Hiranyakashipu, raged with revenge and anger. The king hated Vishnu so much that he tortured Vishnu's followers. To make matters worse, the king was protected by an enchantment given to him by Brahma for the king's previous good deeds. The enchantment ensured that the king couldn't be killed by a god, man, or animal. He would not die on earth or in space, by burning or drowning, during the daytime or the night, indoors or outdoors. In short, his bases were covered. However, this king had a son who refused to turn against Vishnu, much as his father tried to change his son's mind. Angered that his son would not obey him, the king tried to kill his son, and Vishnu decided to intervene as Narasimha (half man, half lion, the fourth incarnation of Vishnu) to destroy the tyrant king before he could hurt his son. As cunning as the king was, Narasimha was smarter. Being part man and part animal, he was able to kill the king during the twilight hours and place his body on his lap above the earth, yet not in space, standing in a doorway. Narasimha recommends that kings should not only be wise but also nice.

VAMANA

(vuh-MUN-uh)

The fifth incarnation of Vishnu is the clever dwarf Vamana. According to legend, Bali, the king of demons, set up shop on earth and gave Indra, the god of the heavens, a pink slip. Wanting to push Bali back into the underworld where he belonged, Vishnu decided he'd need to trick Bali into giving up his new property. So he shrunk down into Vamana's adorable little body and asked Bali if he could have as much land as he could cover in three steps. Looking at Vamana's short legs and tiny feet, Bali agreed, letting out a loud snort. Vishnu then revealed himself to the demon king, transforming from Vamana's diminutive form into that of a giant that kept growing until he was looking down on earth from outer space. Smiling at Bali, Vishnu then took three fateful steps. His first step encircled everything Bali owned in the heavens. His second step covered every square inch of earth. But on his third step, Vishnu rested, allowing Bali and the other demons possession of the underworld. Which just goes to show that you should be nice to small people or they might walk all over you someday.

PARASHURAMA
(puh-ruh-shoo-RUH-muh)

The sixth incarnation of Vishnu is Parashurama, also known as Rama with an ax. His story takes place in a time when the warrior caste known as the Kshatriyas was dishonoring its name by corruption and disrespect to the priest caste, known as the Brahman, whom it was sworn to protect and defend. Luckily a Brahman boy named Parashurama showed more interest in his ax and the art of warfare than in his priestly duties. So, when a battle began after the Kshatriya king stole a priest's magical cow, Parashurama was quick to retaliate with his deadly ax. He destroyed the seven-armed Kshatriya king and his army, sending a clear message to the warrior caste that if it would not protect the Brahman, then the Brahmans would protect themselves. The warrior caste was astonished by the ax-wielding Brahmans and retaliated by killing Parashurama's father. This sent Parashurama and his mighty ax into a horrific rampage of twenty-one battles that wiped out the entire race of warriors. Although Parashurama was victorious, he was struck with great remorse and threw his ax as far away as he could. So don't be fooled; fighting isn't all about glory! Some say that after so much violence done by his own hand, Parashurama disappeared from society and committed the rest of his life to penance on a mountaintop.

RAMA

(RAH-muh)

Vishnu's seventh incarnation is in the form of Rama, who came to earth to destroy the evil king Ravana. Rama is the great hero of the epic story the Ramayana, one of the most beloved stories of India. In the story, Rama is banished from his rightful kingdom of Ayodhya by his wicked stepmother and is sent into exile for fourteen years. While he is away, Rama's wife, Sita, is abducted by the nefarious king Ravana. Hearing the news, Rama sets out on a quest to find his dear wife and conquer the evil tyrant Ravana. Both Rama and Sita are seen as symbols of loyalty and bravery. Lord Rama is celebrated every year in India by a number of festivals, beginning with Rama Navami, which marks his birthday. This is followed by the celebration of Dussehra, ten days of plays that reenact episodes from the Ramayana. Leading up to the grand finale on the tenth day, giant effigies of Ravana, several stories high, are set ablaze, symbolizing the evil king's defeat. And finally comes the festival of lights known as Diwali, thought to commemorate Rama and Sita's return to their kingdom and their coronation. Rama's legacy as the ideal man, husband, and king is an inspiration to millions of Indians every day.

KRISHNA

(KRISH-nuh)

The eighth incarnation of Vishnu is Krishna. His name means both "the dark one" and "all-attractive one." He is considered to be one of the most important and widely worshipped gods in India. In Vishnu's previous avatar, the great king Rama was forever dutiful, following the rules and always serving his kingdom before himself, which is why it is thought that Rama was reincarnated as Krishna: to act out everything that he restrained himself from in his previously proud but boring life. This modest son of a cowherd won the hearts and minds of his devotees by playfully breaking all the rules and by showing generosity of his love. There are many stories of Krishna as a mischievous child. One of his most famous exploits was when his hand got caught in the butter jar, earning him the nickname Maakhanchor (butter thief). As Krishna grew older, he began to steal the hearts of women as well. His favorite pastime as a youth was frolicking with gopis, the girls who looked after the cows. In the evenings, Krishna's flute-playing enchanted them to dance for his pleasure. But no woman was more important to Krishna than Radha. It is said that Radha didn't open her eyes as a young girl until Krishna appeared in front of her. The love between Radha and Krishna developed into the devotional movement known as bhakti yoga, which has come to be known as the Hare Krishna movement.

BUDDHA

(BOO-duh)

The ninth incarnation of Vishnu is Buddha. In the beginning of the present era (Kali Yuga), the Brahman had overburdened the Hindu dogma with pointless rituals and sacrifice that brought more harm than good to its members. Vishnu manifested himself on earth as Buddha and made it his mission to end the Brahman oppression and to purify their rituals. His radical thinking inspired an end to the sacrifice of animals as offerings to the gods. The new doctrines, which he preached as Buddha, taught that everyone could end the cycle of rebirth and attain the state of bliss known as nirvana. Only by practicing and eventually mastering the principles of detachment, mindfulness, and meditation could one hope to overcome the suffering of existence. Buddha was also critical of the Hindu caste system and believed that an individual's karma determined that person's place in society. A bold reformer of Hinduism, Buddha's virtues have spread around the world and continue to attract countless devotees. Many people picture Buddha as a jolly fellow with a potbelly, but he is actually very fit and free from the temptations of society. He is often depicted seated on a lotus, calmly meditating and wearing a simple garment, usually only a robe. During his life, Buddha shared his vast knowledge freely and encouraged people to live in peace, reminding them to keep things simple.

KALKi

(KUHL-kee)

Kalki is the tenth and final Maha Avatar (great avatar) of Vishnu, also known as the avatar of the future. He is to appear at the end of the present age of Kali Yuga (Age of Darkness), when the environment is polluted and society is shrouded in corruption. Only then will Kalki arrive as a one-man army to demolish the imperfect earth. He will appear as a crusader riding a white horse, brandishing a flaming sword, and acting as the final judge and savior of mankind. Kalki doesn't promise any horseback rides to those who let desire, ego, and anger consume them, but he is sure to restore the universal law of order known as dharma. The souls who are spared Kalki's wrath will be purified and go on to start life again in the new era known as the Satya Yuga (Golden Age), marking the beginning of a new cycle of creation. So next time you see a flying horse, it might be a sign to behave better.

HINDU EPICS

The two great Hindu epics are the Mahabharata and the Ramayana. The Mahabharata is a sprawling history of India's ancient dynasties' struggle with one another for land and power. It also explains most of Hinduism's major gods and goddesses. It has been said that everything worth knowing is found within its pages, including the stand-alone portion called the Bhagavad Gita. The Ramayana is more intimate in its scope, primarily following Rama and his small band of devotees in their quest to rescue his wife, Sita. These sacred texts are the cultural foundation of India and the Hindu mythology.

MAHABHARATA

(muh-ha-BAH-ruh-tuh)

The Mahabharata is incredibly long—nearly three times the length of the Bible—and tells the story of the early ancestors of ancient India, the Pandavas and Kauravas, two royal Bharata dynasties, and their ongoing conflicts. The author of this enduring work is the divine sage Vyasa, who was a close companion to both families and so knew their histories intimately. Toward the end of his life, Vyasa decided it was time to dictate the story of the Mahabharata so later generations could benefit from its great lessons. This was a monumental task, as the story spanned hundreds of years of history and mythology. In an effort to find a suitable scribe, Vyasa turned to Brahma for guidance. Without hesitation Brahma dispatched Ganesha, the god of wisdom and the clearer of obstacles, to help with this task. Upon meeting Vyasa, Ganesha pledged his devotion and proclaimed that he would write down the story as fast as Vyasa could recite it. Vyasa agreed so long as Ganesha wrote without error and understood the meaning of what was being said before writing it. Ganesha agreed and in turn challenged Vyasa to recite the story without break until it was complete. Vyasa agreed to Ganesha's terms, and together they began their great task under the shade of a banyan tree. But before they could begin, they needed something to write with, so Ganesha broke off one of his own tusks to use as a pen. This is why Ganesha is depicted with only one tusk (not because of all the sweets he eats).

BHAGAVAD GITA

(BUH-guh-vuhd GEE-ta)

Although the Bhagavad Gita is just a small section of the great epic Mahabharata, it has nearly eclipsed all other sacred texts in Hinduism. *Bhagavad Gita* means "song of the lord" and refers to the message that Lord Krishna conveyed to Arjuna, the great hero of the Mahabharata. A member of the Pandava family, Arjuna was an acclaimed warrior and leader of the Pandava army. At the start of the Bhagavad Gita, he faced a moral dilemma: Should he wage war against his own blood relatives, the Kauravas, with whom he spent his childhood days, or should he risk letting his people down by retreating from combat? On the eve of battle, Arjuna lost his nerve to fight and put the war on hold. Not knowing whom to turn to, he began a conversation with his charioteer, unaware that the driver of his chariot was actually Lord Vishnu in disguise as Krishna. Through their conversation, Krishna convinced Arjuna that he should only concern himself with doing his duty and not with the outcome. To sway Arjuna toward accepting his advice, Krishna revealed his true form. He explained that war would cause the bodies of the slain to be shed off like vessels and that the souls would endure. Krishna declared that there is no shame in doing your duty, and as a member of the Kshatriya warrior caste, it was Arjuna's duty to fight. Lord Krishna restored Arjuna's nerve to begin and eventually win the battle, and in doing so he showed that we must move beyond our own egos and merge with divine consciousness to fulfill our duties. The great peace activist Mahatma Gandhi read the Bhagavad Gita often when he was imprisoned; it kept him committed to his duty and his cause. The Bhagavad Gita and its message of finding mental peace are as useful today as they were 3,000 years ago.

RAMAYANA

(rah-ma-YAH-nuh)

The Ramayana is the second of the two great Indian epics and is a story of devotion and duty. The celebrated hero Rama, Vishnu's seventh avatar, lends his name to the story as it chronicles his journey to save his beloved wife, Sita. Rama was due to take over his father's kingdom of Ayodhya, but he was cheated out of his rightful position when his stepmother, Kaikeyi, exiled him to the forest for fourteen years. Rama honored his stepmother's wishes and took leave of his kingdom. Before leaving, he advised his wife to stay in the palace, away from the hardships of forest life, but Sita insisted on accompanying her husband and remained dutifully at his side. Together with his half-brother, Lakshmana, Rama and Sita fled to the woods. But a little while later, when Rama and his brother were hunting, Sita was abducted by Ravana, the king of the demons. As Rama and Lakshmana searched for Sita, they came across the monkey chief Sugriva and were promised the help of his monkey army, led by the loyal Hanuman. After the fleet-footed Hanuman succeeded in locating the imprisoned Sita on the island of Lanka (modern-day Sri Lanka), they set to work building a land bridge from the tip of India to the island. With the help of the monkey army, Rama defeated both Ravana and his army, Sita was finally rescued, and they returned home victorious. So work hard to do your duty, and if things get tough, it never hurts to ask a monkey for help.

DEMIGODS

Demigods, also known as devas, are gods that have a lower status than the mahadevas (great gods), since they are servants to the supreme god Vishnu. There are many demigods, and they rule everything in the universe from fire, water, and air to love, death, and war. Thus, Hindus consider the entire universe sacred and worthy of worship.

AGNI
(UHG-nee)

Agni is one of the most important of the ancient Hindu gods. He is the god of fire, and his flame is thought to dwell in each of us. Though perhaps not what is intended by the saying "fire in the belly," Agni is also believed to bring us energy and life as we digest our food. It is said that his flame ignites the stars in the sky and brings light to our planet through the sun. Even though Agni was revered by the ancient Hindus and a number of sacred books are dedicated to him, he is not an arrogant god. Agni gives to the poor just as he gives to the rich, warming the hearths of both homes indiscriminately. Agni's flame is used in many Hindu ceremonies, and he has the honor of acting as a conduit between the gods and humans. Something of a messenger boy, Agni carries the prayers of the gods' devotees to the gods themselves after offerings are made to him. To make an offering to Agni, one must present a gift to feed his flame and keep it burning brightly. However, one cannot just make an offering to the god of fire without first consulting a compass. Agni is very particular about which direction he is facing when an offering is made to him. If Agni is facing east, his fire should be used for sacrifices to the gods. When he is facing south, his fire should be used for sacrifices to the spirits of the dead. And be sure that you do not confuse Agni's flame with your cooking fire; that should always face toward the west. It's important to get this right, as you wouldn't want your offerings to the spirits of the dead commingling with your simmering curries. If this is too confusing, just make Agni an offering of ghee (clarified butter). This will keep you in any god's good graces. So next time you burn a little butter, don't feel bad. It might bring some good luck.

INDRA

(IN-druh)

Indra is the god of war and storms, particularly those involving thunder and lightning. In ancient times Indra reigned supreme because he controlled the great celestial weapon, the vajra (lightning). He used the vajra to zap his enemies and to revive those killed in battle—a handy feature in a celestial weapon. In addition, Indra was known to imbibe a special nectar known as soma, the drink of immortality, which would expand his size to gigantic proportions. This helped him battle his enemies and caused him to let out some mean burps. Armed with his power drink and lightning bolt, Indra would ride into battle on the great white elephant Airavata, whose mighty steps shook the ground and echoed like thunder. Indra's most notable exploit was when he went into battle with the demon Vritra, a greedy dragon who got carried away with staying hydrated and drank all the water in the world. Indra was outraged and vowed to take back the liquid of life. Chugging as much soma as he could, Indra let out a fearsome burp as he filled with strength. Thunder boomed across the land as Indra and his powerful elephant charged toward Vritra, ready to pop the dragon demon like a water balloon. As Vritra's stomach was split wide open by Indra's lightning bolt, a deluge of water fell from the sky, ending the years of drought that had plagued the land and its people. Indra became a hero and was crowned the king of all gods, a lofty title but one that was short-lived. Indra's fate was the same as many of the ancient Hindu gods: Over time he lost much of his importance. Eventually, Indra was given the minor role of a weather god, offering up the same forecast of thunder, lightning, and rain.

VAYU

(VYE-yoo)

Vayu is the god of air and wind. He is also known as Pavana (the purifier). He gets around on the back of the nimble antelope, one of the few animals fast and agile enough to keep up with the gale-force winds he unleashes. Vayu is thought to have had many affairs, one of which caused him to father Hanuman, the monkey god. According to legend, once, when the gods were looking for a vacation home, they asked a sage to recommend a place on earth. The sage thought it would be best to create a perfect paradise and so gave careful instructions to Vayu to create a wind so powerful that the peak of Mount Meru, a holy mountain, would blow off and become a sanctified piece of land fit for the gods. Vayu thought he had this one in the bag and began to huff and puff. Unbeknownst to Vayu, the peak of the mountain was protected by Garuda, a bird often seen carrying Lord Vishnu from place to place. Garuda spread his mighty wings and shielded the sacred peak from Vayu's fierce winds for a full year. Eventually Garuda's will and feathers were nearly eroded, and the poor bird was forced to take a rest. As Garuda lowered his tired wings, the sage informed Vayu of the mountain peak's vulnerability. At that moment, Vayu blasted the peak so strongly that the top broke off and went flying clear across India. It landed with a huge splash in the ocean, where it now rests as the tropical paradise of Sri Lanka, a stunning home for any god.

KUBERA

(koo-BAY-ruh)

The dwarf god Kubera has a checkered past. He started as a demon and a known thief. In the great Hindu epic Ramayana, Kubera was accused of abducting Sita. In fact, it was Kubera's brother, Ravana, who did the kidnapping, using Kubera's magical chariot as the getaway vehicle. Guilty by association, Kubera had to work to restore his reputation. Using his special chariot, he delivered jewels and other valuables into the hands of the poor. But Kubera wasn't always so generous. Some believe he was only elevated to the status of a god because he tried to rob a temple devoted to Shiva. During the robbery, Kubera's bumbling ways caused his torch to blow out. He tried again and again to relight it, but to no avail. Finally, on the tenth attempt, he succeeded, but of course he was no closer to stealing anything of value from the temple. Kubera's pathetic attempt to rob the temple amused Shiva, who astonishingly granted the thief immortal status as a god. Who says crime doesn't pay? These days, Kubera uses his knowledge of jewelry heists and bank robberies to guard the earth's treasures. Kubera is depicted with a fat belly, a clear sign of his greedy appetite for wealth. He carries a water jug and a money pouch, and he is never far from Nakula, his pet mongoose, known to spew out jewels—but only into the hands of his master. Who needs a credit card when you have a handy-dandy mongoose to pay for your expenses?

VARUNA

(VUH-roo-nuh)

Varuna is one of several gods who used to be greatly revered, but now serves a much more minor role in Hinduism. Long ago, Varuna reigned over a wide variety of territories: He controlled the movement of the sun in the sky; ensured that the night and day never met, maintained order amongst the gods and goddesses; created rain, sleet, and snow; and was the final word in enforcing contracts between two parties. In short, Varuna had his hands in a lot of pots. He was all powerful and always busy. He rode a sea monster to get around—in and of itself a symbol of his power over land and sea. To help keep order, he had a lasso and a snake. But worship of this overworked god fell off largely due to his mishandling of one of the earth's most precious resources: water. When the demon Vritra drank up all the water on earth, Varuna didn't know what to do. The great god Indra had to intercede to recover what was stolen. Afterward, Varuna was fired as head honcho, and Indra took his place as the supreme god. Since water was Varuna's downfall, he was put in charge of guarding the waters of the earth.

KAMA

(KAH-muh)

Kama is the son of Vishnu and Lakshmi, the god of preservation and the goddess of fortune. He is considered the god of love and desire, so it's no surprise that his mythology reads like a romance novel. Not only is he blessed with eternal youth, but he is also thought to be one of the most handsome gods. He can be seen riding a parrot, the symbol of sensuality, and goes nowhere without his tools of love: the mythical bow and arrow. Kama, similar to the Greek Cupid, shoots arrows of desire that make their intended targets fall blissfully in love. The epitome of romance, Kama is happily married and is accompanied by his wife, known as passion, and his friend, spring. This trinity of love has innumerable stories, but it is Kama's matchmaking skills that have become legend. According to one story, Kama disturbed Shiva when he was deep in meditation by shooting him with his arrow of love. But instead of fanning the flames of passion, Kama unwittingly unleashed the scorching heat of Shiva's ire. With one quick glance from his third eye, Shiva incinerated Kama—but not before Kama's arrow of love had hit its mark, for Shiva fell in love with Parvati, and later the two were happily married. Lots of good that did Kama! He was now dead, and love had died with him. Without love to bring forth new life, it wasn't long before the universe began to die. The gods, fearing extinction, begged Shiva to have Kama reborn. Shiva agreed, and Kama was restored as a son of Krishna, who was no stranger to love. Thus, romance and desire were restored to the universe. But if you want to ask someone out on a date, it's probably not a good idea to shoot them with an arrow—better leave that to the professionals.

KARTTIKEYA

(kar-tih-KAY-yuh)

Don't be fooled by this god's adorable appearance, for he is Karttikeya, the secretary of defense to the gods' armed forces. He is also known as Skanda in the southern states of India, where he is far more popular than in the northern regions. Karttikeya is the poster child of warfare. He's young, brave, and always ready to take up his favorite weapon, the spear. Instead of a tank or destroyer, he rides a peacock. The peacock, though seemingly not a vicious animal, is more than capable of destroying harmful serpents, which represent the ego and bad desires. Karttikeya and his brother, Ganesha, are the sons of the god Shiva and goddess Parvati and accordingly had very special births. Ganesha's birth came when Parvati molded him out of clay. Karttikeya is the creation of Shiva, with a little help from the fire and river gods, Agni and Ganga. According to legend, while Lord Shiva and Parvati were on their honeymoon, having a wonderfully blissful time, the gods were in a panic that a child would be conceived that would be so mighty and invincible that he would topple all other gods. They intended to put a stop to the two lovebirds and interrupted their private union. As a result Shiva's glowing seed was accidentally released into the air. His seed was so bright and luminous that only Agni, god of fire, could carry it. Agni deposited the seed, according to Shiva's directions, in the Ganges River. The goddess Ganga then nourished the seed, causing a living being, Karttikeya, to spring from it.

GANGA

Goddess Ganga was born from one of Vishnu's divine toes. One day, as Vishnu was listening to Shiva play beautiful music, Vishnu's toes began to heat up and started to melt! Hoping to contain the god's melting feet, another god scooped up the liquid, which then became the Ganges River, deemed holy because of its origins. According to legend, the Ganges originally flowed only through heaven. It was due to a mortal, King Sagar, that the river came down to earth. King Sagar had 60,000 sons, each of whom he loved dearly. One day, the king sent his sons out to find his horse, which had been set loose to roam the land months before. As it so happened, the horse came to rest near a sage named Kapila Muni, who was mistakenly thought to have stolen the horse. When the sons confronted Muni, the sage burned them to ashes, trapping their souls on earth. King Sagar was greatly distraught, especially when he learned that his sons' only hope of reaching heaven would be if the sacred river Ganges flowed down to the earth and washed over their ashes. Luckily, King Sagar's great-grandson Bhagirathi was a sage of the good variety and performed rigid penances directed toward Brahma until the god of creation agreed to allow the river to fall to earth. Goddess Ganga was not happy about her relocation and swore that as she descended she would fall with such force that she'd flood the whole world and destroy humanity. To prevent this, Shiva stood under the spot where Ganga fell from the sky and cushioned her fall by using his thick hair as a sponge. Her water was made even more holy by Shiva's contact, and the locks of his hair divided her into seven rivers, which are the Ganges and its tributaries. Eventually the Ganges found its way to King Sagar's sons and sanctified their remains. Ganga is most often depicted tangled in Lord Shiva's hair or as a beautiful goddess riding Makara, a crocodile. Hindus believe that bathing repeatedly in the Ganges' waters cleanses one of sin and secures one's place in heaven.

YAMA

(YUH-muh)

Yama is the god of judgment and death. Knowing everyone's deeds, he imparts justice according to their history and then escorts their souls to their final judgment in hell or heaven, thus keeping earth tidy and free from lingering spirits. Yama rides an intimidating black buffalo, a form that he also adopts from time to time when he needs to sneak up on his victims. In one hand, he wields a noose, with which he snatches hold of his prey; in the other, he holds a mace, which represents the weapon of punishment. Yama did not begin as a god. He earned his title by being the first human to die and thus the first to learn about the path of the dead. Yama's death had an unexpected consequence. After Yama died, Yami, his twin sister, went into an inconsolable sadness. Her grief was so great that it began to threaten the entire universe. Since Yama and Yami were the first humans to test out creation, the gods had never run into this problem before. They quickly realized that they had forgotten to create the passage of time, making it impossible for Yami to reach an end to her grieving. The gods' simple solution was to create night, thus bringing the passage of time into being. Over time Yami was able to move beyond her grief, and creation was once again restored. Another of Yama's more useful traits is his tendency to bonk you over the head to help you forget your emotional pain.

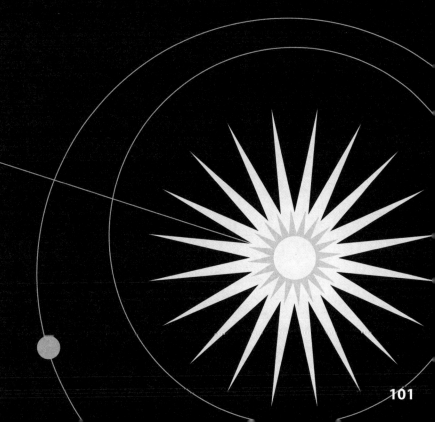

NINE PLANETS (Navagraha)

In the Indian solar system, there are nine planets that are believed to influence and affect Hindus in their daily lives. The nine planets are called Navagraha, *nava* meaning "nine" and *graha* meaning "planets." Hindus have ascribed a rich mythology to each of the planets and have determined what positive and negative impacts they have upon one's life, depending upon their position in the sky and the temperament of the planet. By using Hindu astrology and birth charts, an individual can determine what might occur in his or her life and what needs to be done in order to offset one's bad karma developed during a former life or to develop good karma in the present life.

SURYA

(SOOR-yuh)

Since ancient times, millions of Hindus have started their day by chanting the Gayatri Mantra, a greeting to the great sun god Surya, also known as Savita. Repeating the holy mantra directed toward this god is believed to bring success and salvation and can help one attain a place in heaven. Surya is known as "the one who enlightens and stimulates understanding." The role of Surya is very similar to that of Brahma, the god of creation. Surya is thought to preserve life on earth through his nourishing rays, his warmth, and his light. Each day, Surya rides across the sky in a golden chariot drawn by seven white horses, one horse for each day of the week. The chariot is driven by the god of sunrise, a hero of Hindu legend named Arjuna. Sometimes Surya is depicted with two hands, each holding a lotus, the symbol of creation. Sometimes he has four hands, one holding a lotus, another a conch shell, another a chakra, and the last hand held in a gesture of protection. It's not safe to stare at the sun, but if you look quickly, you might see him flashing you a peace sign.

CHANDRA

(CHUN-druh)

The moon, known as Chandra, is the second most important planetary god. Similar to how Lakshmi, the goddess of wealth, was born, the moon emerged from the sea of milk when it was being whipped into a frenzy by the demons and gods. When Chandra rose from the milky water, he nearly blinded the gods and demons with his powerful luminosity. Not owning sunglasses, the gods unanimously decided that Chandra should be sent to live in the cosmos and given the status of a planet. Perhaps if the moon were less weak-minded, he could have argued for a place among the gods. Instead, he packed his bags and set up shop in outer space. From there, Chandra moved from one disastrous affair to another. His first lover, Tara, was the wife of his guru Brihaspati. From their illicit union, the planet Mercury was born. He was named Budha and hated his father immediately, as his birth was the result of a deadly sin. From this hatred, a rivalry sprung between the moon and his son, which continues to this day. As time progressed, Chandra's deeds went from bad to worse as he set out to marry the twenty-seven daughters of Daksha, an ancient god. Daksha granted Chandra permission to marry his many daughters under the condition that the moon not favor one daughter above the rest or else he would suffer the consequences. But Chandra failed to keep his promise and was cursed to lose his divine luster, which is the cause of the moon's waxing and waning. Despite Chandra's checkered past, he is considered one of the best planets to be born under and promises wealth and happiness. Perhaps this is because he is associated with soma, an intoxicating drink known to dazzle even the most ferocious of the gods.

MANGALA

(MAHN-guh-luh)

The red planet, Mars, is considered one of the worst planets to be born under, as it is known as Mangala, the god of warfare. He is an aggressive god, often associated with Karttikeya (the god of war), the violence brought about through war, and the sacrifices necessary to satisfy the greater good. He has four hands, two of which hold the weapons of war, generally a bow and a javelin, while the other two are held in positions of protection and blessing. He can be seen charging into battle atop a forceful ram. Though a ferocious god and something of a hothead, Mangala isn't without virtue. He is known for his valor, strength, resolve, and courage. He is also known to offer protection to the weak and weary, and he serves as the guardian of dharma, the sacred path each of us must follow through life.

GURU

(GOO-roo)

The planet Jupiter is known as Guru or Brihaspati. He is the teacher of the gods and so is one of the most important planets. Guru's wardrobe is made up mostly of yellow and gold-colored robes, which he is often seen wearing while sitting on a lotus like a wise sage. His teacher's salary affords him a golden crown, wishing wand, and a fine rosary for his meditation. The worship of this planet can cure stomachaches, clean up sins, and improve your grade point average, as he is the source of vidya (good education). Thursdays are considered to be the best day to worship Guru, and if you find yourself eating channa dhal that day, consider setting some aside for this great teacher, because apples won't win you any brownie points. Guru recommends that everybody, including the gods, pay attention to their teachers, or else you might get a stomachache.

BUDHA

(BOO-duh)

Brahma, the god of creation, named the planet Mercury "Budha" in honor of the planet's sharp intellect. But don't confuse this wise planet with Buddha the enlightened sage; the only thing they have in common is their names. Those who are born under this planet have a definite edge should they choose to pursue a career in education or business, as they are known to be efficient, funny, and literate. They also get to leave their calculators at home since they are savvy in mathematics as well. Budha bears a striking resemblance to the handsome god Vishnu, which is a cause for some confusion as, in order to earn Budha's respect, it is quite common for people to pray to Vishnu instead. Unlike some gods, Budha doesn't seem to mind sharing the spotlight and will take your prayers however you choose to give them. We generally see him depicted with four hands and riding upon a chariot or a lion. Three of his hands hold a sword, a shield, and a mace, while the fourth one is held in a blessing gesture. A prayer to Budha, especially on Wednesdays, brings blessings of fertile lands and juicy tomatoes.

SUKRA

(SOOK-ruh)

If Guru is the teacher of the gods, Sukra is his polar opposite. Associated with the planet Venus, Sukra is the spiritual tutor to the demons. He finds himself quite busy protecting the demons from their long list of enemies and resurrecting the dead using his excellent memory for magical formulas. Although this planet is smart, once in a while he miscalculates and bad things happen. For example, one time he turned himself from a two-eyed god into a one-eyed god. According to legend, Sukra was helping Bali, the king of the demons, perform a fire ceremony. During the ceremony, Vamana (Lord Vishnu in the guise of a dwarf), asked the king for a small gift. Sukra was immediately suspicious of the dwarf and advised King Bali not to entertain Vamana's request. But the king, thinking he knew better than his tutor, disregarded Sukra's advice. In accordance with Hindu custom, he lifted a jug of water in order to pour it on the ground, a necessary step to show he has authorized the gift. Sukra foresaw the king's action and quickly recited a magic formula so he could enter the water invisibly to prevent it from falling. But Vamana was one step ahead of Sukra. He rammed a straw into the basin of water, which caused Sukra to lose an eye. The water thereupon fell, and the gift was ratified. Those born under this planet will have the handy ability of knowing the past, present, and future.

SHANI

(SHUH-nee)

Saturn, known as Lord Shani, has possibly the worst reputation amongst the planets. For those unlucky enough to be born under his influence, a life of pain and misery awaits. In fact, many dread Shani's power, not just those born under him, as he's been known to rid Hindus of their wealth in order to teach them a harsh lesson about karma. Some Hindus even refuse to do business during periods of Shani's orbit in order to avoid his influence. This planet's reputation began to sour when he accidentally caused Lord Ganesha's head to fall off, an interesting variation from the legend of Shiva cutting it off. Even for a god, it's difficult to recover from something like that! Saturn earned another bad mark when his half-brother became angry with him and stabbed him in the foot, causing him to limp. As such, he is known as the slowest of the nine planets. According to Hindu mythology, Shani is the son of Surya (the sun) and Chaya (the sun's "shadow wife"), and it is believed that Chaya's shadow element is what makes Shani so harmful. On the bright side, under Shani's influence a person's character is strengthened—he teaches us how to overcome our hardships through hard work and taking responsibility. In a bittersweet way, he brings about bad things in order to motivate a person to change. It has been said that Saturn disciplines us until we can learn to discipline ourselves. When Shani is not limping from one place to the next, he rides the crow, which is thought to protect him against thieves.

RAHU

(RAH-hoo)

Rahu is classified by Hindu astronomers as a planet, but really he should be thought of as an "eclipse" demon. Legend has it that after a great flood covered the world, the gods and demons got together to help each other find some of the precious items that were submerged in the water. One such item was amrita, the nectar of the gods. Rahu, a demon, disguised himself as one of the gods and quickly stole a drink of the precious liquid. Once the drink passed his lips, Rahu became immortal, and just in time, for within seconds, the sun and moon detected the fraud. They shouted to Lord Vishnu for help. Vishnu turned to where Rahu stood and launched his chakra from the tip of his finger. With blinding speed, Vishnu's wheel severed Rahu's head from his body. But the nectar had already been swallowed, assuring Rahu and the severed parts of his body immortality. His head was transferred to the solar system, where periodically Rahu takes revenge on the sun and moon for squealing on him by swallowing them up, which we know to be solar and lunar eclipses.

KETU

(KHET-oo)

Ketu is an imaginary planet. According to Hindu mythology, Ketu represents the tail of the eclipse demon, Rahu. The two planets are parts of the same demon, made immortal through trickery and speed but busted for theft by the sun and moon. Rahu, the head of the demon, is forever angry and plotting his revenge on the tattletale gods. This is in perfect contrast to Ketu, who was cut off from Rahu by Lord Vishnu's chakra. Since he has been touched by Lord Vishnu, however indirectly, Ketu is thought to be in a perpetual state of bliss. With his chill demeanor, he is considered to be more detached from the world's desires, while Rahu is still toiling to exact revenge, always angry due to his worldly concerns and bruised ego. Still, Ketu doesn't mind helping Rahu when it comes time to get back at the sun and the moon. Together, they periodically swallow them, causing solar and lunar eclipses. Because Ketu and Rahu are able to blacken these two bright globes, they are considered the most powerful influences in the zodiac. Truth be told, Ketu would rather just hang out with Lord Vishnu; but don't tell his other half!

ANIMAL GODS

Hindus believe that gods reside in all living creatures. In fact, many gods and goddesses manifest themselves as animals or have divine creatures as their means of transport. Animals are so omnipresent in Hinduism that many gods are symbolized by their respective animal. The god Krishna's symbol is the docile cow, and king cobras are the symbols of Shiva and Vishnu, while the elephant-headed Ganesha is the perfect hybrid of animal and god. Through this interweaving of gods and nature, the ancients cultivated a deep respect for animals and learned to coexist with them.

NAGAS

(NAH-guhs)

Nagas, or snakes, have been honored since ancient times in India. According to Hindu belief, snakes have a dual identity: They are at once semidivine and semidemonic. Sacred snakes are thought to wrap their coils around the earth's treasures, ensuring their constant protection. They have also come to symbolize the infinity of creation, as snakes miraculously shed and regenerate their own skin. But, in their demonic aspect, nagas appear as part human and part snake, as in the case of the demons Rahu and Ketu. Nagas are also often depicted with several heads, such as Vasuki, the snake king, who used his serpent body as a rope to help the gods during their quest to churn the oceans. The god Vishnu also rests in the coils of a great multiheaded snake known as Sesha. To further sanctify nagas, they were once thought to have sheltered the meditating Buddha during a great storm by surrounding the wise monk with the coils of their bodies and forming an awning with their hoods. Controlling many aspects of water, such as rivers, lakes, and rainfall, snakes have come to symbolize life and fertility.

GARUDA

(GUH-roo-duh)

Garuda is the king of birds. He can move from one world to another at the speed of light, which makes it easy for him when he must relay messages between the gods and humans. Garuda is half bird, half man, and is often seen with wings, talons, and a beak, while his body, arms, and legs are human. He also has quite an appetite. As soon as he poked his head out of the shell from which he was born, he wanted to eat. His dad sent him off to a small village to find food (meaning he could eat the people who lived there). But he warned Garuda, "Do not eat the Brahman." Garuda, in his haste, however, swallowed the Brahman, who got lodged in his throat. Scared to disobey his father and murder a Brahman, let alone choke to death, Garuda spit the Brahman and villagers out. This left Garuda very hungry and frustrated. But unbeknownst to him, Vishnu had been watching. Approaching Garuda, Vishnu asked if Garuda would like to perch on his arm and eat from his flesh. Awed that when he bit into Vishnu, he left no visible marks, Garuda realized he was in the presence of a god and pledged his lifelong allegiance to him. So it's not uncommon to see Vishnu soaring through the sky on Garuda's back. If you are lucky, someday you may find one of Garuda's feathers.

HANUMAN

(HUH-noo-muhn)

Hanuman, the son of Vayu, the lord of winds, is also known as the monkey king. He has the head of a monkey and a muscular human body, with the special ability to expand to the size of a mountain or shrink down to the size of a fly. He is often depicted flying in the air while carrying a mountain single-handedly, which is a reference to his role in helping his friend Rama during his great battle with Lord Ravana, as chronicled in the epic Ramayana. When Ravana injured Rama's younger brother, Lakshmana, on the battlefield, Hanuman flew to the mountains to retrieve healing herbs. Unsure which herbs to pick, Hanuman returned with the entire mountain. When he was sent as Rama's envoy, Hanuman was given a ring to convince Sita that he truly was her husband's messenger. With a formidable leap, he crossed the seas and reached Lanka (known today as Sri Lanka), where Sita was being held captive. He succeeded in relaying Rama's message to Sita and went on to help build a bridge from India to Lanka, enabling Rama's army to free Sita. In addition to being strong and clever, Hanuman is a loyal and faithful friend. When was the last time someone brought you a mountain?

SURABHI

(SOO-ruh-bee)

The mythical mother of all cows is Surabhi. She is seen as a symbol of abundance and generosity, and she helps purify our bodies, blessing us with good health and prosperity. Cows are of great importance, as they take care of many of our needs. Not only do they provide milk for children and adults, their by-products of yogurt, buttermilk, and butter are an integral part of the daily Indian diet. Their dung is a useful year-round fuel supply and is a tool in agriculture and rural development. Even after death, their skins are reclaimed and used for leather goods. India celebrates the sacred cow through worship of one of its favorite gods, Krishna, also known as Govinda (cowherd) and Gopala (protector of cows). Krishna loved the taste of fresh butter and kept a cow as a symbol of his kindness. To guarantee that this valuable resource is not abused or mistreated, Hindus give cows a very special place in Indian society, that of a sacred mother—they cannot be harmed under any circumstance. Through religious significance and cultural laws, Hindus have made sure the humble cow is protected and venerated as a powerful symbol of nonviolence and the respect Hindus have for all animals. Remember, without cows we wouldn't be able to enjoy our favorite snack, cookies and milk.

CHRONOLOGY of CREATION

In the beginning, while Vishnu slept in the infinite coils of the great serpent Sesha, it is thought that he dreamt up the creator god, Brahma, who emerged from Vishnu's navel already seated upon a perfect lotus flower. Brahma then began the work of creation, starting with the four yugas (great ages) known as Satya (Krita) Yuga, Treta Yuga, Duapara Yuga, and Kali Yuga. Each of these ages repeats 1,000 times in each cycle of creation, known as a Kalpa, which is then followed by the disillusion of the universe, known as Pralaya. It is believed that this all takes place within Vishnu's dream, which is our reality. Thus, everything we know is maya (illusion), or merely a figment of Vishnu's imagination.

1

SATYA (KRITA) YUGA
(Age of Truth)

The first quarter of the creation cycle is known as the golden age of perfection and harmony.

3

CHURNING of the OCEANS
Both gods and demons cooperate to churn the cosmic oceans to recover the gifts lost during the previous disillusion of the universe.

4

LOST TREASURE
The churning of the cosmic waters yields great gifts: the sun and the moon; the gods of earth, fire, wind, and water; the great goddess Lakshmi; the white elephant Airavata; and a divine cow and horse.

7

VAMANA OUTWITS BALI
Vamana, an avatar of Vishnu, tricks the demon king Bali out of his kingdom on earth and heaven. Vamana also blinds Bali's advisor Sukra in one eye and drives the demons down to the underworld.

1

MANU and the FLOOD

Before the beginning of our time, there was an end of an age. Pralaya, the end of creation, was imminent, so to ensure that knowledge and mankind would survive, Vishnu descended to earth as his first avatar, Matsya, to save Manu and the Vedas from destruction.

2

BRAHMA, CREATOR

Brahma begins another cycle of creation. He creates the universe and everything in it, including gods and demons, using Vishnu's body as the substance of creation.

5

STOLEN AMRITA

After finding the lost nectar of immortality, the demon Rahu manages to steal a sip. He pays dearly for this, as Vishnu severs him into two undying beings, Rahu and Ketu.

6

VRITRA, DEMON OF DROUGHT

Indra slays the dragon Vritra with the use of his lightning weapon known as vajra, and he recovers the water stolen from the world.

2

TRETA YUGA

(Age of Reason)

The perfection age comes to an end, which marks the beginning of the less-than-ideal age in the second quarter of the world cycle.

8

PARASHURAMA RAMPAGE

The Brahman priest Parashurama punishes the warrior caste for its corruption and lack of honor.

9

HONORABLE RAMA

Vishnu's seventh avatar, Rama, destroys evil in the form of Ravana, a demon king. His legend lives on because of the rich example he set for following one's duty, honor, and dharma.

10

HANUMAN, LOYAL COMMANDER

The clever monkey-man known as Hanuman saves Rama's brother during battle and leads his army to victory.

3

DUAPARA YUGA
(Age of Greed)
During the third quarter of the world cycle, greed and the ambitions of kings burden the earth.

11

KRISHNA, LOVER of LIFE
With the charm of his flute and his playful spirit, Vishnu's eighth avatar, Krishna, teaches men and women to let go of their greed and anger.

12

MAHABHARATA
The epic war between two great dynasties of the Pandavas and the Kauravas for the throne and kingdom ruled by the Kuru clan.

13

BHAGAVAD GITA
Krishna, disguised as Arjuna's charioteer, advises Arjuna to follow his dharma and to lead his army to victory.

4

KALI YUGA

(Age of Darkness)

Today we live in the final quarter of the world cycle, characterized as the age of chaos and moral breakdown.

14

ENLIGHTENED ONE

Vishnu's ninth avatar is Buddha, the great purifier of Hinduism and preacher of contemplation and compassion.

15

FUTURE AVATAR

Vishnu's final avatar, Kalki, is said to appear during the final days of this age to act as judge and savior.

16

PRALAYA

The disillusion of the universe arrives, signaling the start of another cycle.

1

SATYA (KRITA) YUGA

A new cycle of perfection and harmony begins, and hope is once again restored to humanity.

Don't worry,

ghee happy

Nap
time

GLOSSARY

Asura: Beings that are considered demonic and mortal enemies of the devatas.

Brahman: The Hindu priesthood caste.

Chakra: Ancient symbol of the sun and cycles of life. As a disc, it is a powerful weapon and a common attribute of Lord Vishnu.

Devatas: The gods that work to protect and control the universe.

Dharma: A philosophy and code of conduct that emphasizes religious duty and honor.

Ghee: Clarified butter used as a fuel for holy fires.

Holy Vedas: Ancient set of text for conducting religious rituals and prayers to the Hindu gods.

Kala: Time, or related to the god of death.

Kalpa: One cycle of creation.

Karma: A belief that positive events are the results of positive past deeds in previous lives.

Lingam: A sacred stone symbol of Lord Shiva.

Maharishi: One who has mastered his mind, body, and soul, and is considered enlightened.

Maya: Illusion, or the things that bind us to our desires.

Nirvana: A state of liberation from the mind and body.

Pralaya: The disillusion of the universe, also known as Brahma's night.

Puja: A Hindu religious ceremony.

Shakti: Strength or power personified as Devi, the great goddess.

Trimurti: The holy trinity of Hindu gods, comprised of Brahma, Vishnu, and Shiva.

ACKNOWLEDGMENTS

Sanjay Patel is an animator and storyboard artist at Pixar Animation Studios. He spends a lot of time looking for taquerias that will serve him french fries along with his burritos. He was born in England and raised in L.A. but has never been to India. Sanjay and his wife left the country once to go to Italy and found a hole-in-the-wall restaurant in Florence that served french fries on top of fried eggs.

To my wife, **Manisha**, thank you for carrying my contact lens case and splitting milk shakes with me. There was no way this book could have been made without your eyes and your good taste. I must have asked you to look at this stuff a gazillion times until you said those magic words, "Oh, that's cute."

The most mellow New Yorker that I never met, my patient editor, **Emily Haynes**. Thank you for gracing this book with your editorial wisdom and sensitivity. You patched up my literary weaknesses and taught me about the all-important em dash.

With respect to my fabulous agent **Tina Wexler** at ICM, whom I've met through particles of DNA that she sends along with contracts. Thank you for discovering my artwork in the abyss of cyberspace and finding a home for it at Plume.

Brace Man, thanks for being a pal and believing in this book from the very start. **Ern** and **Zen**, thank you for your friendship and support with this project.

To my buddies **Billy**, **Dan**, and **Toaster,** thanks for all the laughs, and to all my friends in the animation department ghetto, keep smoothing out those splines.

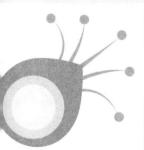

Big thanks to the **Afterworks** crew. Without the support and excitement of a group of us all doing books together, I wouldn't have made it this far.

To my Adobe InDesign gurus, **Mr. Giglio** (www.superfunfun. com), **Mr. Boyd**, **Mr. Dreyfus**, and **Mrs. Hill**, you're all design lifesavers.

Rinky Baby, thanks for untangling the mess I made on the Web. **Mrs. Charu**, thanks for teaching me my Hindi ABC's. **Mr. Rosenast**, you're always there with the funny ideas free of charge.

To all my teachers: **Julie Tabler**, thank you for taking me under your wing and starting me on my path. **Mr. Sonnenburg** (www.conducthappiness.com), thanks for showing me how to airbrush an eye and telling me about CalArts. **Kevin** and **Jill**, I can't think of two better people to learn the joy of animation from.

To the illustrators who dazzled my eyes, my sincere apologies if I've stared too long: **J. Otto**, **Richard Scarry**, **Saul Steinberg**, the **Provensens**, and **Mary Blair**.

To all my **Guju** friends and family, it's hard to stay in touch and create things like this. Thanks for your love and support; now, go rent some rooms.

OM SHANTI (praise peace)
The scared syllable Om (Aum) is considered the main symbol of Hinduism and is revered as a holy mantra. *Shanti* simply means "peace." This phrase is how Hindus have begun and ended their teachings for thousands of years.